NEPHI AND LEHI
IN PRISON

To Patrea, with much love

Sherrie Johnson

To my wonderful son, Carson, with love

Tyler Lybbert

Printed in Mexico.

10 9 8 7 6 5 4 3 2 1

ISBN 0-87579-857-8

Designed by Craig Geertsen.

NEPHI AND LEHI
IN PRISON

WRITTEN BY
SHERRIE JOHNSON

ILLUSTRATED BY
TYLER LYBBERT

DESERET BOOK COMPANY
SALT LAKE CITY, UTAH

The people of Nephi had become so stiff-necked that they refused to be governed by law or justice. This iniquity made Nephi, the chief judge, weary. There were more people who chose evil than good! Filled with concern, Nephi yielded up his judgment seat so he could spend the remainder of his days teaching his people.

Stiff-necked means "stubborn."

Stubborn people are called stiff-necked because they won't turn to see anything but what they want to see.

Together with his brother Lehi, Nephi preached from one city to another until they had gone forth among all the people of Nephi. Then they continued southward to Zarahemla to teach the Lamanites.

Nephi and Lehi were the sons of Helaman.

Helaman named them after the Lehi and Nephi who came out of Jerusalem about 570 years before this time.

In Zarahemla they preached with such great power and authority that eight thousand of the Lamanites were baptized unto repentance.

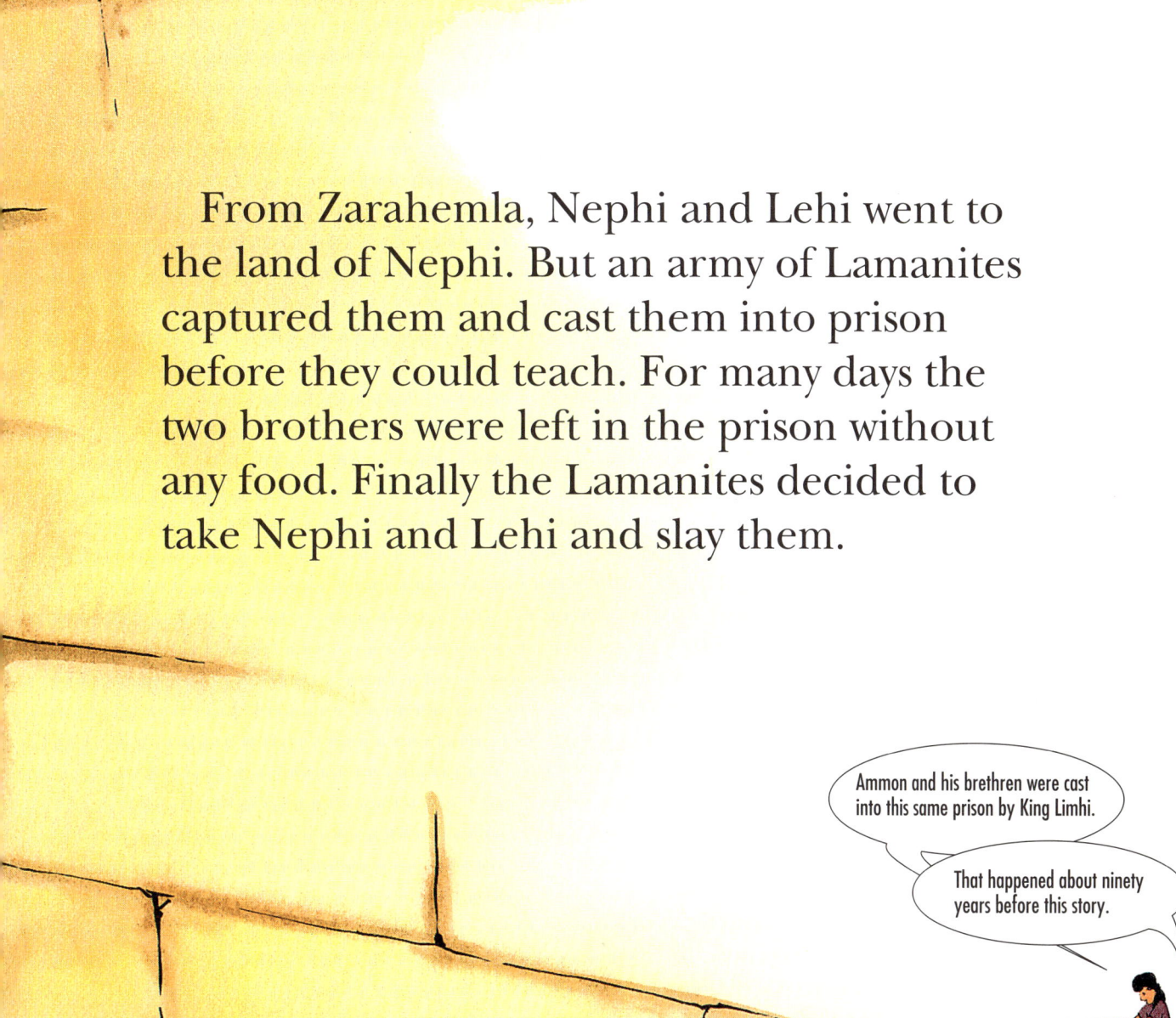

From Zarahemla, Nephi and Lehi went to the land of Nephi. But an army of Lamanites captured them and cast them into prison before they could teach. For many days the two brothers were left in the prison without any food. Finally the Lamanites decided to take Nephi and Lehi and slay them.

Ammon and his brethren were cast into this same prison by King Limhi.

That happened about ninety years before this story.

But when the Lamanites entered the prison, Nephi and Lehi were encircled about by fire. The men were astonished and dared not lay their hands upon the prisoners for fear of being burned.

When Nephi and Lehi saw that they were protected by a pillar of fire, their hearts took courage. They saw that the Lamanites stood as if struck dumb with amazement.

"Fear not," the brothers said, "for behold, it is God that has shown unto you this marvelous thing."

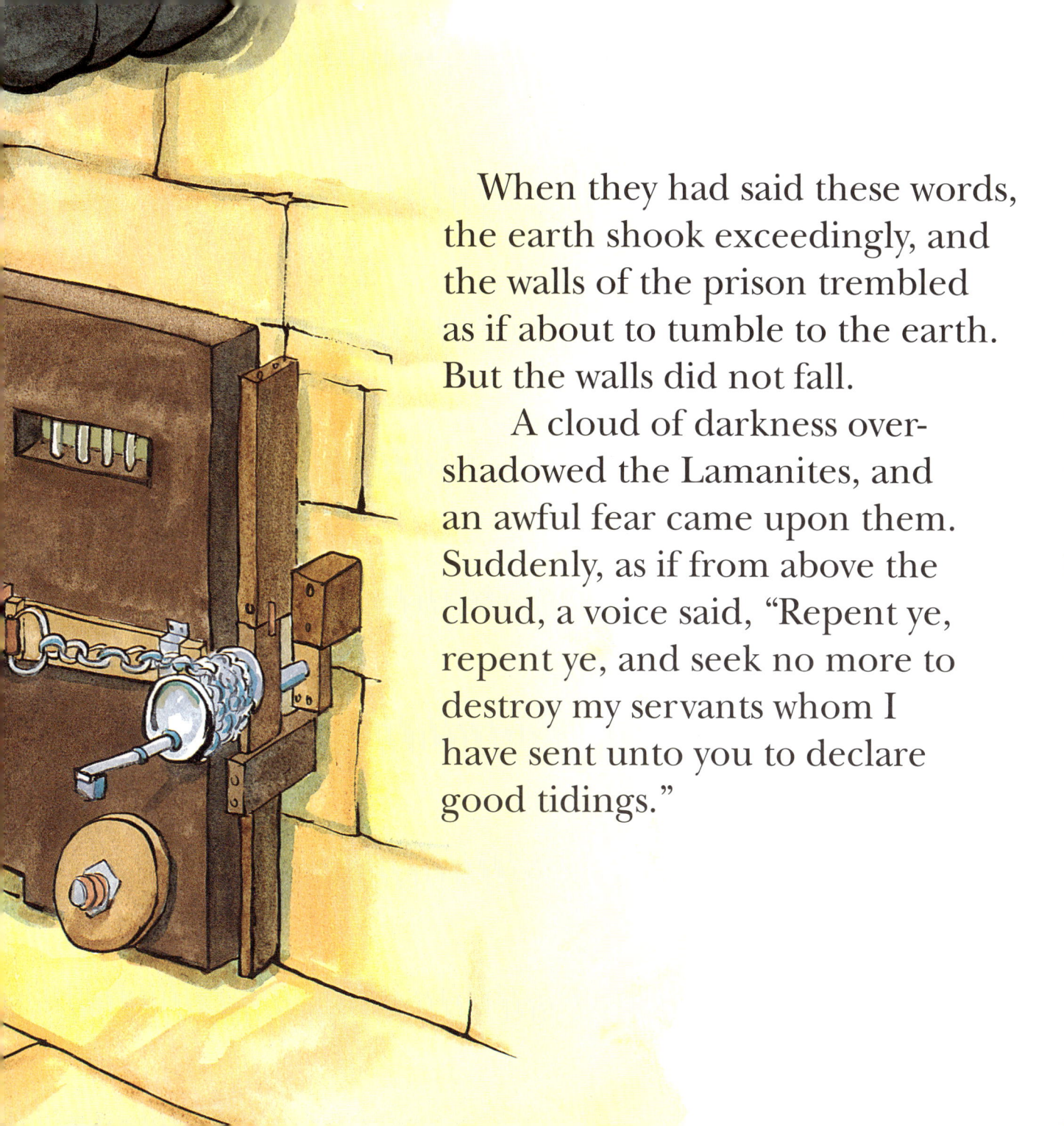

When they had said these words, the earth shook exceedingly, and the walls of the prison trembled as if about to tumble to the earth. But the walls did not fall.

A cloud of darkness overshadowed the Lamanites, and an awful fear came upon them. Suddenly, as if from above the cloud, a voice said, "Repent ye, repent ye, and seek no more to destroy my servants whom I have sent unto you to declare good tidings."

The voice was not a voice of thunder or great tumultuous noise. It was a still voice of perfect mildness, like a whisper, and it did pierce even to the very soul. But notwithstanding the mildness of the voice, the earth shook again, and the walls trembled again. And the cloud of darkness, which had overshadowed them, did not leave.

Tumultuous means "violent." And *not-with-standing* is three words put together to make one long word.

Notwithstanding is used a lot in the Book of Mormon.

It means "in spite of."

"Repent ye, repent ye, and seek no more to destroy my servants," the voice said again, and once more the earth shook and the walls trembled.

Then a third time the voice whispered. This time it spoke marvelous words that cannot be uttered by man. Again the walls trembled, and the earth shook as if it were about to divide asunder. But the Lamanites could not flee because of their fear.

Divide asunder means "break into parts."

Now there was one among them who was a Nephite by birth. His name was Aminadab, and he had once belonged to the church of God but had dissented. He turned and saw through the cloud of darkness that the faces of Nephi and Lehi shone exceedingly, even as the faces of angels. Their eyes were lifted to heaven, and it was as if they were talking to someone.

"Look!" Aminadab cried to the multitude. They turned and saw the faces of Nephi and Lehi.

What does *dissented* mean?

It means Ah-MIN-ah-dab refused to obey the laws of the gospel.

"Behold, what do all these things mean?" the Lamanites asked. "And who is it with whom these men converse?"

Aminadab answered, "They converse with the angels of God."

"What shall we do that this cloud of darkness may be removed from us?"

"You must repent," Aminadab said, "and cry unto the voice, even until ye shall have faith in Christ, who was taught unto you by Alma, Amulek, and Zeezrom. When ye shall do this, the cloud of darkness shall be removed from overshadowing you."

Converse means "talk."

AL-ma, AM-you-lehk, and Zee-EZ-rum were prophets.

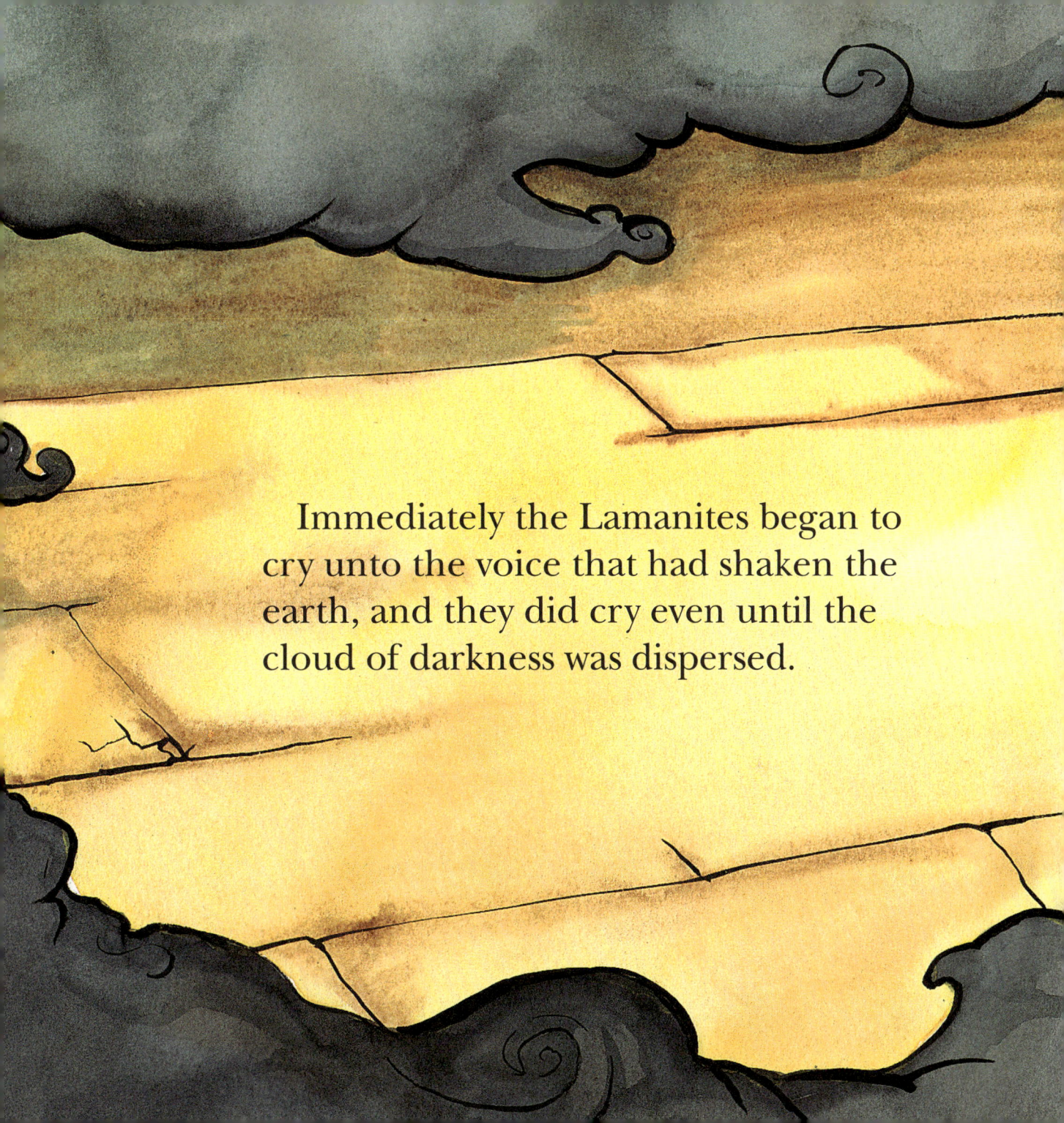

Immediately the Lamanites began to cry unto the voice that had shaken the earth, and they did cry even until the cloud of darkness was dispersed.

When the cloud was dispersed, they saw that they were encircled about, every one of them, by a pillar of fire. But the fire did not harm them, nor did it burn the walls of the prison. And the men were filled with joy.

Then the Holy Spirit of God came down from heaven and entered into their hearts. They were filled as if with fire, and they spoke marvelous words.

Once more the voice whispered unto them, "Peace, peace be unto you because of your faith in my Well Beloved, who was from the foundation of the world."

When they heard this, they looked in the direction of the voice and saw the heavens open, and angels came down and ministered unto them.

After that day the men went forth and taught their people. They declared unto them all they had heard and seen while in the prison. Because of this, many of the Lamanites were converted and laid down their weapons of war and their hatred and the wicked traditions of their fathers. They gave back to the Nephites the lands they had taken in war, and they lived the rest of their lives in peace.

If you want to read this story yourself, you'll find it in Helaman, chapter 5.